CW00530992

GERMANY

Michael G. Burns

Front cover illustration: One Tornado GR.1 from each of the four Laarbruch interdiction/strike and reconnaissance squadrons formate shortly after the last Jaguar GR.1 squadron to convert, No 2, became operational on the type. At the front is a No 16 Squadron aircraft, identified by the 'Saint' image, black outlined gold bar, and gold crossed keys on a black disc. Next, the distinctive stripes and the aggressive cheek-borne squadron badge – an eagle brandishing a sword against the rising sun – identify a No 20 Squadron machine. No 15 Squadron uses the Roman 'XV' rather than Arabic numerals in its designation and incorporates this in its badge. On the pinnacle aeroplane, No 2 Squadron's bars and tail code base echo the triangles identifying artillery reconnaissance and contact machines in the First World War. The obscure position of the RAF serial number on Tornadoes is irritating. The subtle variations in camouflage pattern are noteworthy. (RAFG Laarbruch)

Back cover illustration: Puma HC.1s of No 230 Squadron take part in an infantry exercise. During the late 1970s the replacement of the ageing Wessex by the Puma enhanced RAFG's ability to transport troops and equipment within and around the battlefield.

▲1

1. Time-sequence of RAF Bruggen Tornado GR.1s crossing the runway threshold at the end of a practice bombing sortie. (Sgt G. Card, ABIPP, RAF Bruggen)

RAF GERMANY

Michael G. Burns

ARMS AND
ARMOUR

▲2 ▼3

2. A No 31 Squadron Canberra PR.7 at Laarbruch during Exercise 'Royal Flush' in 1965, being towed from dispersal by an airfield tractor. (No 31 Squadron Association)

3. Part of No 3 Mobile Field Photographic Unit (MFPU) and a No 31 Squadron Canberra PR.7 at De Peel air base, Holland, the detachment for War Alert. The photograph was taken by the oblique camera of another of the squadron's Canberra PR.7s. The trailers are for processing, printing and viewing the film. No 3 MFPU was a permanent attachment to No 31 Squadron. (No 31 Squadron Association)

4. A camouflaged No 31 Squadron Canberra PR.7, WT513, low over the German countryside, photographed by another of the squadron's PR.7s. Until 1959 the squadron did mainly high-level PR work – hence overall PR Blue finish – with a fan of six F52 and one F49 vertical cameras. From 1959 the squadron did both low- and high-level PR, with F52s and the new F95 cameras, and wore tactical camouflage. (No 31 Squadron Association)

▼4

INTRODUCTION

First published in Great Britain in 1990 by Arms and Armour Press, Artillery House, Artillery Row, London SW1P 1RT.

Distributed in the USA by Sterling Publishing Co. Inc., 387 Park Avenue South, New York, NY 10016-8810.

Distributed in Australia by Capricorn Link (Australia) Pty. Ltd, P.O. Box 665, Lane Cove, New South Wales 2066, Australia.

British Library Cataloguing in Publication Data
Burns, Michael G.
RAF Germany. – (Warbirds fotofax)
1. West Germany. Great Britain, Royal Air Force. Squadrons
I. Title   II. Series
358.4'131'094-1
ISBN 0-85368-918-0

Designed and edited by DAG Publications Ltd. Designed by David Gibbons; edited by David Dorrell; layout by Cilla Eurich; typeset by Typesetters (Birmingham) Ltd and Ronset Typesetters Ltd; camerawork by M&E Reproductions, North Fambridge, Essex; printed and bound in Great Britain by The Alden Press Ltd, Oxford.

At the forefront of NATO's deterrent forces, RAF Germany (RAFG) would play a critical role in the event of war in Europe. It forms parts of NATO's Second Allied Tactical Air Force (TWOATAF), which provides air support for Northern Army Group (NORTHAG) in the critical Allied Forces Central (AFCENT) European Area Command. RAFG undertakes a full range of tactical roles and is entirely at the 'sharp end' – 99 per cent of its aircraft are combat types and it is prepared for immediate offensive and defensive combat operations.

The European defence alliance was constructed under Article 4 of the Brussels Treaty of 1948 and consolidated by the North Atlantic Treaty, signed in 1949, creating NATO. The multi-national forces of NATO's Allied Command Europe (ACE) are deployed against the Warsaw Pact's forces from northern Norway to southern Turkey in three Area Commands: North (AFNORTH); Central (AFCENT); and South (AFSOUTH). Each is divided into sub-commands in which operations are the responsibility of an Army Group (AG) supported by an Allied Tactical Air Force (ATAF).

AFCENT, the most critical, covers all of West Germany, Belgium and the Netherlands, and part of the North Sea. It is divided along a north-east Liège-Gottingen axis into Southern Sector with CENTAG and FOURATAF, and the more vulnerable Northern Sector with NORTHAG and TWOATAF. TWOATAF comprises West German, Dutch and Belgian elements, based in their own countries; US Air Force Europe (USAFE) elements; and RAFG. With headquarters in Holland, its commander is usually the RAFG commander.

In 1969 an assurance, given to NATO by the British Government that the UK's air power assets would be primarily devoted to NATO, became effective. Since the RAF withdrew from colonial duties, RAFG has been the UK's main overseas air power commitment. With Headquarters at Rheindahlen, RAFG has operated four bases since then: Bruggen, Laarbruch and Wildenrath, the 'clutch airfields', and Gütersloh; it also has a presence at Berlin-Gatow.

RAFG is a self-contained air force. Its major commitments are providing nuclear strike, conventional attack, interdiction, ground support, reconnaissance and air defence forces for NATO air operations, and for the immediate support of land operations in the NORTHAG area, in co-ordination with TWOATAF units.

As a multi-national deterrent force, NATO adopts a defensive posture. Thus, defensive forces only are designated as NATO assets assigned to the Supreme Allied Commander Europe (SACEUR). Offensive forces remain under national control until a stage in NATO's threat reaction escalation process is reached, when they too would be assigned to SACEUR.

Under the 1955 Bonn Convention, RAFG discharges a national commitment, like all NATO-assigned formations. Complementary to its NATO air defence commitment, it is responsible for the integrity of the northern half of West Germany's national air space.

Since 1969 RAFG has deployed the full range of RAF combat aircraft to fulfil most modern combat roles. It has re-equipped three times with aircraft and weapons more appropriate to meeting the developing Warsaw Pact threat. The period can be divided into 1969–75, 1975–84 and 1984 onwards.

This book would not have been possible without the RAF's photographers, acknowledged herein, who produce such excellent photographs, nor without the many others who have taken their own photographs over the years, and kindly made them available for the enthusiast. Special thanks are due to Nigel Gillies, MIPR, Senior Information Officer, RAF Germany, and all the RAF Germany bases and squadrons; to Terry O'Halloran and No 31 Squadron Association; Derry East; Wing Commander Dick Bogg; Greg Ferguson and Betty Hornby, British Aerospace; and Sarah Last of Westland for providing photographs. Particular thanks are due to Modeltoys; Maintrack Models; David Cass of Lead Sled; Andrew Deeley of ED Models; Tim Perry of PP Aeroparts; John Short of Airkit Enterprise; Hannants, Lowestoft; for assistance with the modelling information. This book is dedicated to the air and groundcrews who maintain our security in the European frontline, whatever the political climate.

▲5   ▼6

5. In the cockpit of his Lightning F.2 is 'Boss' Gilbert, CO of No 92 Squadron at Geilenkirchen. The others are (left to right, starboard): Armstrong, Richardson, Ayllward, Roberts, McKnight, Stein, unknown, Sqr Ldr Cohu; and (port): Bruce, Lucas, Denny, Rogers, Bowler, unknown, unknown. Note the 30mm Aden cannon tubes in the F.2's nose. (D. East)

6. No 92 Squadron Lightning F.2 XN732 'H', with two Firestreak missiles, wearing 1960s natural metal finish. The squadron emblem is a cobra. The fin and spine are dark blue. Built as an F.2, and first flown in November 1962, XN732 was delivered to No 92 Squadron on 30 April 1963, as 'H'. It was converted to an F.2A from 26 November 1968, returning to the unit on 12 August 1969. Reduced to spares, it went to No 60 MU as 8519M in March 1974. It returned to Laarbruch in December 1976 as a decoy. (D. East)

7. No 92 Squadron Lightning T.4 XM995 'T' still carries two Firestreak AAMs. This aircraft joined No 92 Squadron on 29 November 1962, in the UK. No 92's markings are red and yellow chevrons in a fighter arrowhead, and its fin emblem is the squadron badge, an orange cobra with a brown branch with leaves on a white disc. This latter has lately been worn by its Phantoms, but its chevrons have become checks. (D. East)

8. XV577, an early Phantom FGR.2 of No 31 Squadron at Bruggen, taxies out of its shelter with the canopies and outer wings still raised. It carries the original-style national insignia, squadron markings and gloss grey/green camouflage with large bars on the intake cheeks. From 1969, the entry of the Buccaneers, Phantoms and Harriers into RAFG's service, in the long-range strike/attack, fighter-bomber/strike/attack (FBSA) and close support roles respectively, considerably strengthened the Command's offensive capability. In 1971 Phantoms also became fully operational in the tac-recce roles

with No 2 Squadron, the fourth
Phantom unit. (No 31 Squadron
Association)

9. Phantom XV433 of No 31
Squadron with the squadron's
badge and bars on the nose and
'Star of India' on the fin. It has
the old-style national insignia.
On No 17 and then No 31
Squadrons' Phantoms, the fin
flash was of the raked and tapered
pattern, as here. Serial numerals
in white were painted near the tip
of the fin and, in black, on the
nose wheel front door. In 1972
the white was removed from the
national insignia and flash trim.
XV433 is shown carrying a full
complement of tanks, one
dummy Sparrow and a CBLS
100. (No 31 Squadron
Association)

7▲   8▼

9▼

▲10 ▼11

10. A Phantom FGR.2 three-ship formation of No 14 (XV487), No 17 (XV419) and No 31 (XV433) Squadrons over JHQ RAF Germany (TWOATAF). XV487 still has old-style underwing roundels, retained by No 14 Squadron for some time after the general change to red/blue markings. (No 31 Squadron Association)

11. No 31 Squadron aircrew, including CO Wing Commander Chris Sprent (third from left, standing), pose a variety of clothing with a squadron Phantom. The dual language 'Rescue' label is visible. No 31 Squadron's Phantoms had a gold five-pointed star (mullet) encircled by a medium green laurel wreath with a red bow at the bottom on a white disc flanked by white outlined bars of yellow and medium green checks. Latterly the Phantoms had a simplified nose star in yellow only, and nose checks were outlined in white on some aircraft. (No 31 Squadron Association)

12. Phantom FGR.2 XV393 of a No 31 Squadron detachment to Decimomannu, Sardinia, being serviced. Its wing fuel tanks are grey/green/grey. It carries a CBLS 100 practice bomb-dispenser. The rear ladder is of interest. Front ladders are seldom used on RAF Phantoms. (No 31 Squadron Association)

13. On New Year's Eve at Decimomannu, a member of No 31 Squadron poses to sicken the folks back at Bruggen. The number of stencils on the Phantom FGR.2 is clearly shown All No 31 Squadron Phantoms carried the single-tone yellow star nose marking until April 1976 when the two-tone star with white surround was introduced on Phantoms participating in Exercise 'Royal Flush', held that year. At the same time the groundcrews' names were stencilled in white on the port intake splitter plate. (No 31 Squadron Association)

12 ▲   13 ▼

14. Phantom FGR.2 XV402 of No 31 Squadron with trolley-accumulator plugged in to keep the computers alive. The aircraft carries 370 US gal Sergent Fletcher wing tanks, a 600 US gal centre-line tank – the largest Phantom store other than the RAF EMI recce pod – a CBLS 100 3lb or 4lb practice bomb-dispenser and a dummy Sparrow missile in the left forward recess. (RAFG via No 31 Squadron Association)

15. Semi-matt-camouflaged Phantom FGR.2 XV426 of No 31 Squadron rotates at Bruggen, the undercarriage already going home. The auxiliary air door on the aft fuselage above the engine efflux is open. The old control tower is in the background. The photograph was taken by the navigator of a second Phantom. (No 31 Squadron Association)

▲14   ▼15

16. Phantom FGR.2 XV498 of No 17 Squadron equipped for the FBSA role with the devastating SUU-23/A 30mm Gatling cannon, plus two CBLSs and a dummy Sparrow. No 17 was the second Bruggen FBSA Phantom squadron to form, a month after No 14 in 1970. XV498 was flown by No 17 Squadron between 1973 and 1976. (RAFG)

17. No 31 Squadron Phantom FGR.2 XV476 letting down after a practice run on the bombing ranges. This aircraft flew with No 31 between 1971 and 1976, and then joined No 92 Squadron as a fighter. (No 31 Squadron Association)

18. Line-up of four No 3 Squadron Harrier GR.1s finished in the standard 1970s tactical finish of semi-matt Dark Green/ Dark Sea Grey upper surfaces and Light Aircraft Grey undersurface camouflage, with hard colour demarcations. No 4 Squadron began operating Harriers with RAFG from Wildenrath in 1970, joined there by No 20 Squadron in 1971 and No 3 Squadron in 1972. (BAe)

16 ▲   17 ▼

18 ▼

▲19 ▼20

▼21

19. The pilot of No 3 Squadron Harrier GR.1 XW768 'G' in the hover applies thrust – note the smoke from the rear 'thrust' nozzles, fully opened intake ducts and depressed flaps and lowered undercarriage and air brake. The Harrier's ability to manoeuvre in a hover permits it to land in forested areas such as this or to swing on to the road. 'G' carries rocket pods, a standard Harrier GR.1 weapon. (BAe)

20. No 3 Squadron Harrier GR.1 XW768 'G' lands with the barbed wire stressing the defensive environment in which RAF Germany squadrons operate. The Harriers are very much front-line units. The unit's cockatrice badge is set in a white disc on the nose, flanked by green rectangles edged top and bottom in yellow. The squadron's code letters were and remained yellow. No 3 Squadron has been based in Germany since the end of the war, operating Tempests, Vampires, Sabres, Hunters, Javelins and Canberras. (BAe)

21. No 20 Squadron Harrier GR.1 XV793 'N' set down in a German pasture, the kind of place from which propeller-driven fighters would have operated but in which most modern jets could not live. No 20's badge is on the nose flanked by light blue/red/white/green/light blue bars. (BAe)

22. Four of No 20 Squadron Harrier GR.1s formate for the camera. Wildenrath was too far from the East-West border for the Harrier's spearhead role, so the Harrier Wing was moved to Gütersloh, 65nm (120km) from East Germany. There was inadequate administrative accommodation at Gütersloh, so the Wing was reorganized into two larger squadrons. No 20 Squadron re-equipped in late 1976 with Jaguar GR.1s in the tactical attack role. Its Harriers went to augment Nos 3 and 4 Squadrons, so overall RAFG's V/STOL close support capability was not diminished and attack was increased and improved. (BAe)

23. In 1975–6 Jaguars replaced Phantoms in FBSA and tactical reconnaissance roles. Flying Officer Tim Penn of No 31 Squadron boards his Jaguar GR.1. Features of interest include the rescue panels, the ladder and its attachments, gun fairing and blast tube, underslung CBLS, the complicated yet space-saving undercarriage geometry, and Penn's garb. (BAe WH6738 via No 31 Squadron Association)

24. No 31 Squadron's Jaguar T.2 showing the two seats and canopies. The squadron's Jaguars carried the unit's yellow and medium green check rectangle with the star surrounded by a laurel in a disc on the engine intake sides. The two-seater retains the GR.1's offensive capability. The operational training role is invaluable. Peacetime administrative control of NATO-assigned air forces is retained by national air arms which are responsible for undertaking the training of assigned units and ensuring their readiness for immediate combat operations, and for providing the necessary logistics and administrative support. (No 31 Squadron Association)

▲24 ▼25

25. No 31 Squadron Jaguar GR.1 XX978 stands outside its HAS at Bruggen with a selection of weapons and two ground-handling equipments. In the front row are (left to right) a stand-off 1,000lb HEMC bomb, a 1,000lb HEMC bomb, a 28lb practice bomb and a CBLS 100, ditto right to left. In the second row (from the left) are two BL755 CBUs, two 4lb practice retarded bombs, a CBLS, ditto right to left. Both ground trolleys lift a store up to the wing. The USAF adopted Mark 82 series streamlined bombs while the RAF persisted in using stores designed to fit the Lancaster's bomb-bay. (No 31 Squadron Association)

▼26

26. Showing the Jaguar's stork-like gait to advantage, GR.1 XX970 'DD' of No 31 Squadron taxies in after a sortie carrying practice retarded bombs in the CBLS on the outer pylons. The ventral fins are in uppersurface colours. (No 31 Squadron Association)

27. No 31 Squadron Jaguar GR.1 XX968 starts to roll, with four more preparing to move out. They carry Dark Sea Grey/Light Aircraft Grey ferry tanks with very soft demarcations. The ventral fins are in the undersurface colour. The finish is semi-matt. During the late 1970s a process of 'hardening up' and 'toning down' took place.

Airfield installations, buildings and runways were camouflaged to make an attack pilot's task difficult; hardened aircraft shelters were installed to protect aircraft, and aircraft camouflage was made matt and markings diminutive. (BAe CN4394 via No 31 Squadron Association)

28. The Jaguar in its element, down among the rhubarb. XZ392 'DQ' of No 31 Squadron runs in for a practice attack. The aircraft wears the Dark Green/Dark Sea Grey matt low visibility scheme, on upper and lower surfaces. The Jaguar was derided as 'the poor man's Phantom'. However, the Jaguar is nimble and fast low down, and small and smokeless and thus difficult to see, especially at low level – and it is highly accurate in weapons delivery. It was designed specifically for the European tactical environment, unlike the Phantom. (No 31 Squadron Association)

29. Jaguar 'DQ' is now over the range, travelling fast, and ready to bomb, using the CBLS practice bomb pannier on the forward belly point. (No 31 Squadron Association)

▲30 ▼31

30. Two of No 14 Squadron's Jaguars at 'peacetime low altitude' over the German plain; a third is just in view on the extreme right. They carry an assortment of weapons: 'AM' has two AIM-9D SRAAMs on LAU-7/A rails outboard and four BL755 CBUs paired on twin racks inboard, with a centre-line fuel tank. 'AC' carries jamming equipment outboard – to port, a Westinghouse AN/ALQ-101-10 ECM, and to starboard, a PHIMAT chaff-dispenser pod – and two LGB 500lb bombs inboard. (BAe)

31. Jaguar GR.1 XX959 'CJ' of No 20 Squadron demonstrates the reasons for Matt Dark Green/ Dark Sea Grey camouflage overall – the aircraft spends its time at low level, frequently near-inverted. It carries two LGBs inboard, with AN/ALQ-101-10 on the port outer and PHIMAT chaff-dispenser pod on the starboard outer pylon. The camouflaged fuel tanks and the sheen on the airbrakes are noteworthy. (BAe)

32. No 2 Squadron Jaguar GR.1 XZ111 'A' carrying the specially developed reconnaissance pod on its centre-line pylon. The pod has roll stabilization, infra-red linescan and forward-looking and fan F95 cameras. The navigation and weapons arming (Navattack) computer marks each frame with latitude and longitude and mission details. No 2 Squadron adapted the markings carried by its Hunter FR.10s for its Phantoms and then Jaguars: the squadron badge, a knot device on a white disc, flanked each side by a white triangle, all on a blue rectangle. Its Phantoms carried these on the nose. A white triangle (a memento of the World War One unit marking) was repeated on the fin bearing a black aircraft code. No 2 Squadron was the last RAFG Jaguar unit, flying the final RAFG Jaguar sortie on 16 December 1988, and is now operating Tornado GR.1s. (RAFG)

33. Two air-defence Phantom FGR.2s, 'C' of No 19 Squadron (nearer) and 'X' of No 92 Squadron, photographed at low level. Much of the air threat in Germany is low and fast. On early RAFG Phantoms, white code letters appeared above the fin badge, and the serial numerals were painted in black at the top of the fin. 'X' carries its full AD load: four AIM-7E-2 Sparrow III MRAAMs and four AIM-9D Sidewinder SRAAMs plus the centre-line-mounted SUU-23/A 20mm rotary cannon. The brains of the system are in the nose – the powerful AN/AWG-10A radar and the crew. (RAFG)

34. Phantom FGR.2 XV489 'V' of No 92 Squadron shows the port view of the early semi-matt Dark Green/Dark Sea Grey/Light Aircraft Grey finish. It carries an inert air combat manoeuvring instrumentation (ACMI) AIM-9 body on the port outer missile

32 ▲   **33** ▼

34 ▼

rail and a ballast AIM-7 on the port forward rail. Interceptor forces are an essential part of RAFG's tactical force: the threat from Soviet aircraft to NATO's Central Region is primarily long-range, low-level attack against bases, installations, communications and deployed forces. (No 92 Squadron, RAFG)

35. Phantom XV489 'V' again, flying low over the waves. RAFG is responsible for maintaining the integrity of the northern half of West Germany's national air space. This area includes the buffer zone along the East/West German border (the Air Defence Identification Zone), the corridors to Berlin and, in co-ordination with RAF Strike Command, an area of the North Sea out to meet UKADR. XV489's outer fuel tanks (Dark Sea Grey/Light Aircraft Grey) are more or less a permanent feature, as fuel is consumed rapidly in the low-level fast interceptor role in which RAF Germany Phantoms are used. (BAe)

▲35 ▼36

36. Quick-Reaction Interceptor Forces have long been a feature of RAFG operations, keeping RAFG continually under operational pressure. To meet the increasing threat of the crowded air space of Central Europe, Rear Warning Radar (RWR) pods mounted at the top of the fin began to appear in 1976–7, here seen on Phantom FGR.2 XT901 'B' of No 19 Squadron. At the same time as RWR, Instrument Landing System (ILS) fins appeared. 'B' reveals the starboard side of the early camouflage and squadron markings: white/light blue/white checks on the intake sides and a black/green inverted dolphin, with red 'wings' or 'fins', mounted on a white oval enclosed by a yellow laurel wreath. (No 19 Squadron, RAFG)

▼37

37. No 19 Squadron Phantom 'H' puts down at Bruggen. The length of the uncompressed nose oleo is noteworthy. The Phantoms liberated by Jaguars on strike/attack duties replaced the Lightnings in the interceptor role. Greater radar capability, heavier and more flexible weapon carriage and wider performance made them far more appropriate interceptors than the Lightning for the tight, low-level, multi-target Central European air defence environment of the late 1970s. It was an overdue step. (RAFG)

38 ▲   39 ▼

38. No 92 Squadron Phantom 'U' slows down with the aid of the brake chute. Its colour scheme is now matt – oversprayed matt varnish or resprayed paint – with subdued roundels, squadron checks on the cheeks and badge on the fin; even subdued warning and rescue markings. Under NATO policy in peacetime air defence forces – interceptors and surface-to-air missile units – are assigned to the operational control of SACEUR to support NATO exercises and counter threatened incursions into NATO air space. (No 92 Squadron, RAFG)

39. Phantom FGR.2 XV480 'X' of No 92 Squadron, in air-superiority finish, goes vertical off Cyprus while on Armament Practice Camp (APC) detachment to Akrotiri. The Central Region is ringed by medium- and short-range missile defences and has effective point defence missiles, but interceptors must counter the

low-level intruders, under tactical control. The Phantoms are ageing, but the two RAFG squadrons are scheduled to run until the mid-1990s alongside the new Tornado F.3 interceptors. (RAFG)

40. In the early 1980s, although RAFG's other aircraft retained matt grey/green camouflage, the Phantoms were resprayed in the new and highly efficient semi-matt three-greys air defence scheme. There is minimal stencilling on the all-grey Phantoms compared with the grey/green Phantoms, as shown on XV467 of No 92 Squadron, also revealing the hard demarcation between the two greys of the Sergent Fletcher tank. (M. G. Burns)

40 ▼

41. Close-up of No 92 Squadron Phantom XV467 showing the engine intake cover, the cheek demarcations and slight leading-edge wrap-around of the upper surface colour. The pylons and the LAU-7/A missile rails are Light Aircraft Grey. (M. G. Burns)

42. No 25 Squadron formed on Bloodhound Mks 1 and 2 in April 1969 and moved to RAFG in 1971. It provided the short-range air defence (SHORAD) capability. No 25 disbanded in March 1983. Rapier, which had provided a second layer of quick-reaction missiles, then took over the role fully. (BAe)

▲41 ▼42

43. No 60 Squadron's Hunting Pembroke C.1s have been based at RAF Wildenrath since the squadron re-formed in the communications role in February 1969. This is XK884. The squadron now flies Andover C.1s and CC.2s. (No 60 Squadron, Wildenrath, RAFG)

44. No 18 Squadron, based at RAF Gütersloh, flew the Westland Wessex HC.2 in the tactical support role. Its helicopters were overall Dark Green/Dark Sea Grey with Black two-letter codes (here, 'BM' XR509) and 'Royal Air Force' below the hump. The Wessex HC.2 was a twin-engined development of the HC.1. No 18 was the RAF's first Wessex squadron. It formed and re-equipped with the type on 9 February 1964. When No 72 Squadron formed as the second unit, No 18 moved to RAF

▼43

Gütersloh. It disbanded on the Wessex in December 1980, later re-forming on Chinooks, and was replaced in Germany by No 230 Squadron with Pumas. (RAFG)

45. An infantry section deplanes from Puma HC.1 'DL' of No 230 Squadron. Air mobility is a crucial element in Central Europe's defence. During the late 1970s the replacement of the ageing Wessex by the Puma enhanced RAFG's ability to transport troops and equipment within and around the battlefield. Frequent exercises are conducted by RAFG's Pumas, Chinooks and Harriers in support of I (British) Corps of the British Army of the Rhine. (RAF Gütersloh)

46. Puma HC.1 XW222 'DF' of No 230 Squadron at low level. The Puma's greater loading-carrying ability, speed, quietness and sophistication made it far more appropriate to the evolving European tactical battlefield (despite some shortcomings) than the Wessex. Puma 'D' has the now-standard engine intake filters. The prominence of the riveting is noteworthy. (RAF Gütersloh)

44 ▲   45 ▼

46 ▼

RAF GERMANY SQUADRONS, BASES AND AIRCRAFT

July 1954

Squadron	Base	Equipment
No 2	Wahn	Meteor FR.9
No 3	Geilenkirchen	Sabre F.1, F.4
No 4	Jever	Sabre F.4
No 5	Wunstorf	Venom FB.1
No 11	Wunstorf	Venom FB.1
No 14	Fassberg	Venom FB.1
No 16	Celle	Venom FB.1
No 20	Oldenburg	Sabre F.2, F.4
No 26	Oldenburg	Sabre F.2, F.4
No 67	Wildenrath	Sabre F.1
No 68	Wahn	Meteor NF.11
No 69	Laarbruch	Canberra PR.3
No 71	Wildenrath	Sabre F.1, F.4
No 79	Gütersloh	Meteor FR.9
No 87	Wahn	Meteor NF.11
No 93	Oldenburg	Meteor NF.11
No 94	Celle	Venom FB.1
No 96	Alhorn	Meteor NF.11
No 98	Fassberg	Venom FB.1
No 112	Bruggen	Sabre F.4
No 118	Fassberg	Venom FB.1
No 130	Bruggen	Sabre F.4
No 145	Celle	Venom FB.1
No 234	Geilenkirchen	Sabre F.2, F.4
No 256	Alhorn	Meteor NF.11
No 266	Fassberg	Venom FB.11
No 541	Buckeburg	Meteor PR.10

June 1975

Squadron	Base	Equipment
No 2	Laarbruch	Phantom FGR.2
No 3	Wildenrath	Harrier GR.1A, GR.3, T.4
No 4	Wildenrath	Harrier GR.1A, GR.3, T.4
No 14	Bruggen	Phantom FGR.2
No 15	Laarbruch	Buccaneer S.2B
No 16	Laarbruch	Buccaneer S.2B
No 17	Bruggen	Phantom FGR.2
No 18	Gütersloh	Wessex HC.2
No 19	Gütersloh	Lightning F.2, F.2A
No 20	Wildenrath	Harrier GR.3, T.4
No 25	Wildenrath	Bloodhound 1, 2
No 31	Bruggen	Phantom FGR.2
No 60	Wildenrath	Pembroke C.1
No 92	Gütersloh	Lightning F.2, F.2A
Berlin Station		
Flight	Gatow	Chipmunk T.10
No 431 MU	Bruggen	—

In the early 1970s — the integration of modern air and land power was consolidated by the British forces in Germany. Considerably stiffening RAFG's offensive capability, Buccaneers, Phantoms and Harriers entered service in strike/attack, fighter-bomber/strike/attack (FBSA) and close support roles respectively. Phantoms took over tactical reconnaissance roles. Lightnings continued to provide the interceptor force. Bloodhound surface-to-air missiles (SAMs) now provided the short-range air defence (SHORAD) capability.

July 1979

Squadron	Base	Equipment
No 2	Laarbruch	Jaguar GR.1, T.2
No 3	Gütersloh	Harrier GR.3, T.4
No 4	Gütersloh	Harrier GR.3, T.4
No 14	Bruggen	Jaguar GR.1, T.2
No 15	Laarbruch	Buccaneer S.2B
No 16	Laarbruch	Buccaneer S.2B
No 17	Bruggen	Jaguar GR.1, T.2
No 18	Gütersloh	Wessex HC.2
No 19	Wildenrath	Phantom FGR.2
No 20	Bruggen	Jaguar GR.1, T.2
No 25	Wildenrath	Bloodhound 1, 2
No 31	Bruggen	Jaguar GR.1, T.2
No 60	Wildenrath	Pembroke C.1
No 92	Wildenrath	Pembroke FGR.2
Berlin Station		
Flight	Gatow	Chipmunk T.10
No 431 MU	Bruggen	—

In the late 1970s RAFG became a co-ordinated air force with a full range of roles and appropriate aircraft with which to carry out its missions. Jaguars replaced Phantoms in FBSA and reconnaissance roles. Phantoms assumed the interceptor role. The Puma replaced the ageing Wessex, enhancing RAFG's battlefield transport capability. A 'hardening up/toning down' process, including introduction of the Rapier SAM to airfield defence, made bases harder to see and penetrate.

January 1981

Squadron	Base	Equipment
No 2	Laarbruch	Jaguar GR.1, T.2
No 3	Gütersloh	Harrier GR.3, T.4
No 4	Gütersloh	Harrier GR.3, T.4
No 14	Bruggen	Jaguar GR.1, T.2
No 15	Laarbruch	Buccaneer S.2B
No 16	Laarbruch	Buccaneer S.2B
No 17	Bruggen	Jaguar GR.1, T.2
No 18	Gütersloh	Wessex HC.2
No 19	Wildenrath	Phantom FGR.2
No 20	Bruggen	Jaguar GR.1, T.2
No 25	Wildenrath	Bloodhound 1, 2
No 31	Bruggen	Jaguar GR.1, T.2
No 60	Wildenrath	Pembroke C.1
No 92	Wildenrath	Phantom FGR.2
Berlin Station		
Flight	Gatow	Chipmunk T.10
No 431 MU	Bruggen	—

July 1984

Squadron	Base	Equipment
No 2	Laarbruch	Jaguar GR.1, T.2
No 3	Gütersloh	Harrier GR.3, T.4
No 4	Gütersloh	Harrier GR.3, T.4
No 9	Bruggen	Tornado GR.1
No 14	Bruggen	Jaguar GR.1, T.2
No 15	Laarbruch	Tornado GR.1
No 16	Laarbruch	Tornado GR.1
No 17	Bruggen	Jaguar GR.1, T.2
No 18	Gütersloh	Chinook HC.1
No 19	Wildenrath	Phantom FGR.2
No 20	Bruggen	Jaguar GR.1, T.2

No 31	Bruggen	Jaguar GR.1, T.2
No 60	Wildenrath	Pembroke C.1
No 92	Wildenrath	Phantom FGR.2
No 230	Gütersloh	Puma HC.1
Berlin Station Flight	Gatow	Chipmunk T.10
No 431 MU	Bruggen	–

No 16	Wildenrath	Rapier
No 26	Laarbruch	Rapier
No 37	Bruggen	Rapier
No 63	Gütersloh	Rapier

Re-equipment since the early 1980s has been slower, but RAFG will be a much more potent force when it is completed. The multi-role Tornado has replaced The Jaguar and Buccaneer in FBSA and recce. roles. The elderly Phantom will serve with the Tornado interceptor until the mid-1990s. Chinooks have endowed RAFG with a previously lacking heavy vertical lift transport capability. While Harrier GR.5 is eagerly awaited for the close-support inventory, the GR.3 soldiers on.

July 1986

Squadron	Base	Equipment
No 2	Laarbruch	Jaguar GR.1, T.2
No 3	Gütersloh	Harrier GR.3, T.4
No 4	Gütersloh	Harrier GR.3, T.4
No 14	Bruggen	Jaguar GR.1, T.2
No 15	Laarbruch	Tornado GR.1
No 16	Laarbruch	Tornado GR.1
No 17	Bruggen	Jaguar GR.1, T.2
No 18	Gütersloh	Chinook HC.1
No 19	Wildenrath	Phantom FGR.2
No 20	Bruggen	Jaguar GR.1, T.2
No 31	Bruggen	Jaguar GR.1, T.2
No 60	Wildenrath	Pembroke C.1
No 92	Wildenrath	Pembroke FGR.2
No 230	Wildenrath	Puma HC.1
Berlin Station Flight	Gatow	Chipmunk T.10
No 431 MU	Bruggen	–

July 1988

Squadron	Base	Equipment
No 2	Laarbruch	Jaguar GR.1, T.2
No 3	Gütersloh	Harrier GR.3, T.4
No 4	Gütersloh	Harrier GR.3, T.4
No 9	Bruggen	Tornado GR.1
No 14	Bruggen	Tornado GR.1
No 15	Laarbruch	Tornado GR.1
No 16	Laarbruch	Tornado GR.1
No 17	Bruggen	Tornado GR.1
No 18	Gütersloh	Chinook HC.1
No 19	Wildenrath	Phantom FGR.2
No 31	Bruggen	Tornado GR.1
No 60	Wildenrath	Pembroke C.1
No 92	Wildenrath	Phantom FGR.2
No 230	Wildenrath	Puma HC.1
Berlin Station Flight	Gatow	Chipmunk T.10
No 431 MU	Bruggen	–

RAF Regiment
HQ No 33 Wing		
No 1	Laarbruch	Light armour
HQ No 4 Wing		

AIRCRAFT SPECIFICATIONS

British Aerospace Harrier GR.3

Type:	Single-seat close support fighter
Powerplant:	Rolls-Royce Pegasus 103 vectored thrust turbofan
Maximum Thrust:	21,500lb (9,760kg)
Dimensions:	
Fuselage length (laser nose)	45ft 7.8in (13.91m)
Height	11ft 4in (3.45m)
Wing span	25ft 3in (7.70m)
Wing area	201.1sq ft (18.68m^2)
Chord:	
Root	11ft 8in (3.56m)
Tip	4ft 1½in (1.26m)
Thickness/Chord:	
Root	10%
Tip	3.3%
Sweep:	
Leading edge	40%
Quarter chord	34%
Tailplane span:	13ft 11in (4.24m)
Fuel Capacity:	
Internal:	
5 × fuselage tanks	
2 × wing tanks	5,510lb: 630 Imp. gal (2,865 litres)
External:	
combat tanks	1,600lb: 2 × 100 Imp. gal
ferry tanks	5,600lb: 2 × 320 Imp. gal
Weights:	
Basic operating with crew	12,300lb (5,580kg)
Maximum take-off	25,000lb (11,340kg) plus
Wing loading, max.	25lb/sq ft (610kg/m^2)
Internal fuel	5,000lb (2,270kg)
Ejection Seat:	Martin-Baker Mk 9A
Performance:	
Maximum speed, Low	737mph (1.186km/h)
Initial climb, VTOL weight	50,000ft (15,240m)/min
Time to height	12,200ft (4,000m) from VTO: 2min 22.7sec
Service ceiling	50,000ft (15,240m)
Range, with one FR	3,455 miles (5,560km)
Tactical radius, internal fuel, Hi-Lo-Hi	260 miles (418km)
Armament:	
Guns, external	2 × 30mm Aden, podded
Air-to-air missiles	2 × AIM-9G, L
Points:	
Normal max. load	5,300lb (2,400kg)
Centre; Inboard × 2	2,000lb (907kg) each
Outboard × 2	650lb (295kg) each
Tips: AIM-9 rail	220lb (110kg)

Weapons:	1,000lb HE bombs, AGM-45 Shrike ARM, BL755, Paveway LGB, rocket pods, flares, 5-camera recce belly pod

Hawker Siddeley Buccaneer S.2B

Type:	Two-seat strike bomber
Powerplant:	Two Rolls-Royce Spey RB.168-1A Mk 101 turbofans
Maximum thrust:	11,100lb st (5,035kgp)
Dimensions:	
Fuselage length	63ft 5in (19.33m)
Height	16ft 3in (4.95m)
Wing span	44ft 0in (13.41m)
Wing area	514.7sq ft (47.82m^2)
Weights:	
Empty	30,000lb (13,610kg)
Loaded, typical	46,000lb (20,865kg)
Maximum take-off	62,000lb (28,125kg)
Fuel Capacity:	
Internal:	
8 × fuselage tanks	1,560 Imp. gal (7,090 litres)
Optional:	
1 × weapon bay	440 Imp. gal (2,000 litres)
1 × bomb door	450 Imp. gal (2,050 litres)
External:	
underwing FR tank	140 Imp. gal (640 litres)
2 × drop tanks	500 Imp. gal (2,275 litres)
Performance:	
Maximum speed	M=0.85 at 250ft (75m)
	M=0.92 at 30,000ft (9,150m)
Normal cruise	M=0.75 at 3,000ft (905m)
Tactical radius:	
Hi-Lo-Lo-Hi	500–600 miles (800–950km)
Hi-Lo-Hi	1,150 miles (1,850km)
Ejection Seat:	Martin-Baker Mk 6MSB
Armament:	
Maximum load	16,000lb (7,257kg)
Missiles	Bullpup, AS.37 Martel ARM
Weapon-bay	4,000lb (1,815kg)
Stores	5 × 1,000lb bombs multi-sensor pack
4 × Wing points	3,000lb (1,360kg) each
Stores	LGB Paveway (Pave Spike Designator), HE bombs, BL755, Rocket Pods, AN/ALQ-101-10 ECM pod, etc.

SEPECAT Jaguar GR.1

Type:	Single-seat tactical support fighter
Powerplant:	Two Rolls-Royce Turbomeca Adour Mk 104
Maximum thrust, each:	
dry	5,260lb st (2,385kg)
reheat	8,600lb st (3,900kg)
Dimensions:	
Fuselage length	50ft 11in (15.52m)
including probe	55ft 2½in (16.83m)
Height	16ft 0½in (4.89m)
Wing span	28ft 6in (8.69m)
Wing area	258.33sq ft (24m^2)

Chord:	
Root	11ft 9in (3.58m)
Tip	3ft 8½in (1.13m)
Quarter chord sweep:	40%
Aspect ratio:	3.12
Weights:	
Empty	15,432lb (7,000kg)
Normal take-off	24,150lb (11,000kg)
Maximum take-off	34,600lb (15,700kg)
Maximum wing loading	126.3lb/sq ft (604kg/m^2)
Fuel Capacity:	
Internal:	
4 × fuselage tanks	
2 × wing tanks	924 Imp. gal (4,200 litres)
External:	
2 × wing, 1 × belly	264 Imp. gal (1,200 litres) each
Ejection Seat:	Martin-Baker Mk 9
Performance:	
Maximum speed	M=1.1 at sea-level
	M=1.5 at 36,000ft (11,000m)
Take-off, typical load	1,900ft (580m)
Landing speed	132mph (213km/h)
Landing run, typical load	1,545ft (470m)
Range, ferry, external tanks	2,614 miles (4,210km)
Tactical radius, internal fuel	
Hi-Lo-Hi	407 miles (815km)
Lo-Lo-Lo	357 miles (575km)
Armament:	
Guns, internal	2 × 30mm Aden cannon
Missiles	Martel AS.37 ARM; AIM-9G, 'L
Stores points:	
maximum weight	10,500lb (4,765kg)
1 × belly	2,000lb (1,000kg)
2 × inner wing, each	2,000lb (1,000kg)
2 × outer wing, each	1,000lb (500kg)
Weapons:	8 × 1,000lb HE bombs, BL755 CBU, Beluga CBU, rocket pods, recce pod

Panavia Tornado GR.1

Type:	Two-seat all-weather strike/attack bomber
Powerplant:	Two Turbo-Union RB.199-34-04 turbofans
Thrust, service max.:	
dry	8,090lb st (3,670kgp)
reheat	15,950lb st (7,235kgp)
Dimensions:	
Fuselage length	54ft 9½in (16.70m)
Height, fin top	18ft 8½in (5.70m)
Wing span	
fully spread, 25°	45ft 7¼in (13.90m)
fully swept, 68°	28ft 2½in (8.60m)
Tailplane span	22ft 3½in (6.8m)
Weights:	
Empty, equipped	30,870lb (14,000kg)
Loaded, no stores	45,000lb (20,400kg)
Maximum take-off, loaded	60,000lb (18,150kg)
Ejection Seats:	2 × Martin-Baker Mk 10A zero-zero

Performance:

Maximum speed:	M=1.2 at sea-level; M=2.2 at altitude
Service ceiling	50,000ft (15,250m)
Tactical radius, Lo-Lo-Hi, 8,000lb (3,630kg) load	860 miles (1,390km)

Armament/Cargo:

Guns	2 × 27mm IWKA-Mauser cannon
Missiles	4 × AIM-7E-2 or Sky Flash MRAAM
	2 × AIM-9G, 'L SRAAM
	4-9 × ALARM
Stores, max. weight	18,000lb (8,150kg)
Hardpoints	3 × belly and 4 × wing
Weapons	AS.30, AS.37 Martel, BL755, 1,000lb bombs, Lepus flare bombs, ECM pods, JP233, Sky Shadow ECM, 500-kiloton nuclear bomb, ALARM, BOZ 107 chaff/flare dispenser, MW-1, Harpoon

McDonnell Douglas Phantom FGR.2

Type:	Two-seat all-weather fighter
Powerplant:	Two Rolls-Royce RB.168-25R Spey Mk 203 turbofans
Military power, each dry	12,250lb (5,556kg) at sea-level
Maximum power, each reheat	20,515lb (9,305kg) at sea-level
Maximum power, each reheat	12,800lb (5,805kg) 36,08ft (11,000m)

Dimensions:

Fuselage length	57ft 7.1in (17.554m)
Height, fin tip	16ft 1.0in (4.902m)
Stabilator span	16ft 5.1in (5.006m)
Wing span	38ft 4.9in (11.706m)
Wing area	530sq ft (49.237m^2)
Aspect ratio	2.82:1

Weights:

Empty	30,918lb (14,023kg)
Basic T-O gross, clean	46,785lb (21,220kg)
Combat gross, Air Defence	41,489lb (18,818kg)
Ejection Seats:	Martin-Baker Mk 7

Performance:

Maximum speed	M=2.2 at 36,098ft (11,000m)
Acceleration	M=0.9 to 2 at 36,089ft (11,000m) 3.17min
T-O over 50ft (15.24m)	2,070ft (16,581m)
Rate of climb, sea-level	
military	13,020ft/min
maximum	45,600ft/min (13,899m)
Ceiling	
supersonic	54,400ft (16,581m)
subsonic	51,500ft (15,697m)
Approach speed	133 knots
Landing ground roll with brake chute	2,350ft (716m)

Armament:

Guns	SUU-23/A 20mm rotary cannon
Missiles	4 × AIM-7E-2 Sparrow III MRAAM or
	4 × Sky Flash MRAAAM
	4 × AIM-9D, 'L Sidewinder SRAAM

De Havilland Canada Chipmunk T.10

Type:	General duty
Powerplant:	De Havilland Gipsy Major 8
Maximum power:	145bhp

Dimensions:

Fuselage length	25ft 8in (7.82m)
Height	7ft 1in (2.16m)
Wing span	34ft 4in (10.46m)

Weights:

Empty	1,417lb (642kg)
Normal loaded AUW	2,000lb (910kg)

Performance:

Maximum speed, sea-level	138mph (222km/h)
Rate of climb, sea-level	800ft (245m)/min
Normal cruise	119mph (191km/h)
Service ceiling	16,000ft (4,900m)
Range clean	292 miles at 124mph (400km at 200km/h)
Endurance	2.3 hours

HELICOPTERS

Westland Wessex HC.2

Type:	Medium tactical transport
Powerplant:	Two coupled 1,350hp Bristol Siddeley H.1200 Gnome turboshafts
Maximum power, total	2,700shp; 1,550shp at rotor head

Dimensions:

Rotor diameter	56ft (17.07m)
Fuselage length	50ft (15.24m) over filter
Height	16ft 2in (4.93m)

Weights:

Empty	7,800lb (3,538kg)
Maximum take-off, gross	13,500lb (6,124kg)

Performance:

Maximum speed	132mph (212km/h)
Range	478 miles (770km)
Cargo:	16 fully armed troops

Aérospatiale/Westland Puma HC.1

Type:	Tactical transport
Powerplant:	Two Turmo IIIC4 turboshafts
Maximum power	1,328shp

Dimensions:

Fuselage length	46ft 1½in (14.06m)
Height	17ft (5.18m)
Rotor diameter	49ft 2½in (15m)

Weights:

Empty	7,180lb (3,255kg)
Loaded, normal	13,220lb (5,995kg)
Loaded, maximum	14,100lb (6,395kg)

HARRIER GR.3, RAF GUTERSLOH, 1989
TACTICAL WRAP

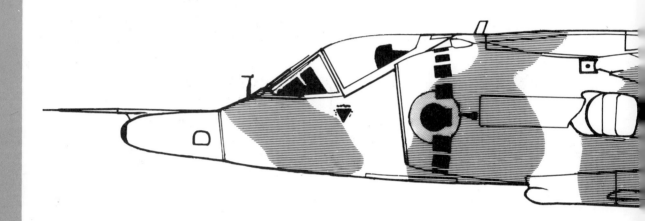

PHANTOM FGR.2D, RAF WILDENRATH, 1989
LOW VISIBILITY MARKINGS

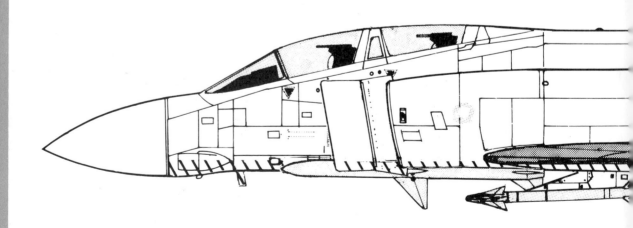

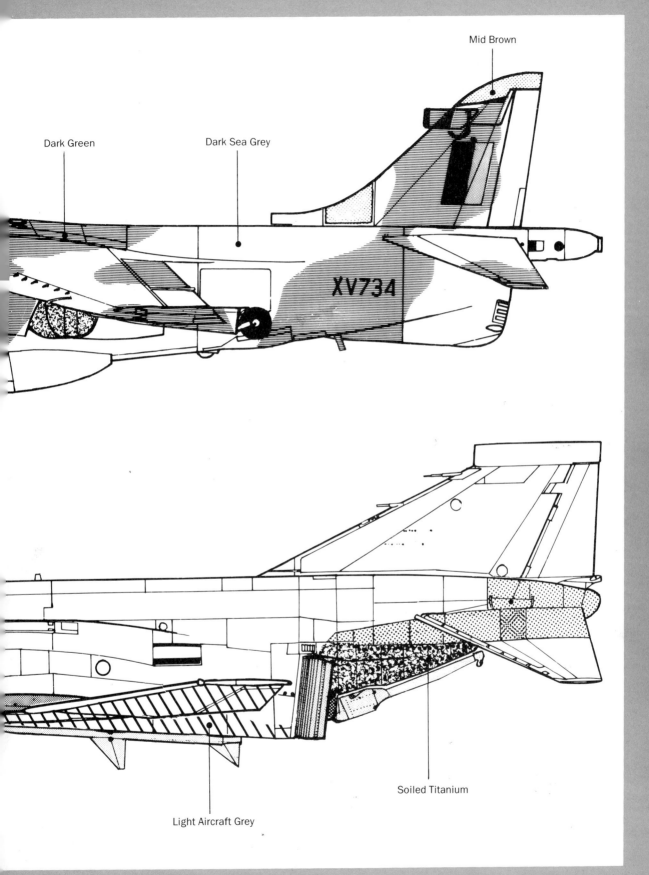

Mid Brown

Dark Green

Dark Sea Grey

XV734

Soiled Titanium

Light Aircraft Grey

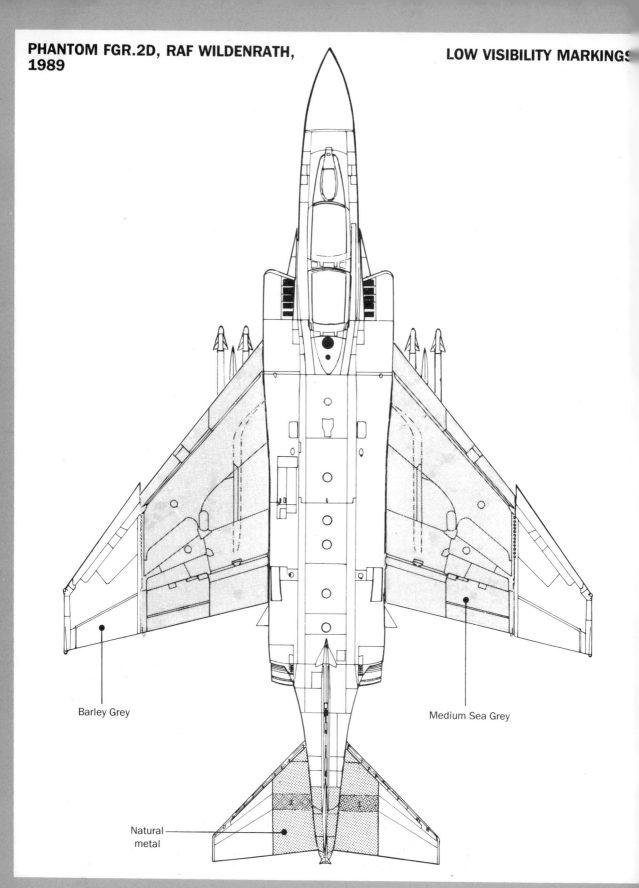

Barley Grey

Medium Sea Grey

Natural metal

Performance:
Maximum speed,	
sea-level	174mph (280km/h)
Maximum rate of climb	2,640ft (805m)/min
Maximum cruise	168mph (270km/h)
Normal cruise	155mph (250km/h)
Hovering ceiling	
In ground effect	14,750ft (4,500m)
Out of ground effect	13,125ft (4,000m)
Range, normal	357 miles (575km)
Cargo:	16 fully equipped troops

Boeing-Vertol Chinook HC.1
Type:	Logistic support, tactical transport
Powerplant:	Two Lycoming T55 turboshafts
Maximum power, each	3,750shp
Dimensions:	
Fuselage length	51ft (15.54m)
Height, top rear rotor hub	18ft 7.8in (5.68m)
Rotor diameter	60ft (18m)
Rotor chord	2ft 1¼in (0.64m)
Weights:	
Empty	21,464lb (9,736kg)

Normal T-O, internal load	33,000lb (14,968kg)
Maximum take-off	50,000lb (22,700kg)
Overload T-O, internal load	45,400lb (20,593kg)
Fuel capacity, internal	1,042 US gal (3,944 litres)
Performance (design gross weight):	
Maximum speed	189mph (304km/h)
Rate of climb, inclined	2,880ft/min (878m/min)
Normal cruise	150mph (254km/h)
Service ceiling	15,000ft (4,570m)
Hovering ceiling	13,600ft (4,145m)
Ferry range on internal fuel	372 miles (600km)
Tactical radius	115 miles (185km)
Payload:	
Crew	Four
Internal	Up to 44 troops or 30 troops seated; or 24 stretchers
Underslung capacity:	
Centre hook	28,000lb (12,700kg)
Forward + rear hooks	20,000lb (9,072kg)
Loads	Fuel containers, field gunds, palleted stores, light tanks, etc.

RAFG PHANTOM CAMOUFLAGE

Tactical Camouflage
The RAF's Phantom FGR.2 (F-4M), originally deployed in tactical roles, were all delivered in 1968—69 in the then standard RAF tactical disruptive camouflage of gloss Dark Green and Dark Sea Grey upper surfaces and Light Aircraft Grey under surfaces. Red/white/blue Type A roundels were carried in the standard six positions, above and below the outer wing panels and on the intake sides. The fin flashes were red/white/blue, in equal widths and initially square, but later raked or tapered, or raked *and* tapered, and sometimes with a white outline.

With the general tone-down of RAF tactical camouflage, Phantoms were resprayed in matt colours from about 1972—73 when they underwent major overhauls, with red/blue Type B roundels created by painting out the white in the Type A roundels. Some, however, retained Type A roundels underwing for several months after the others had been resprayed. Fin flashes also became red/blue, and tapered and raked, similar to the style already adopted by some squadrons.

In both the gloss and matt tactical schemes, the upper surface colours wrapped around the wing leading edges by about 4 inches on to the lower surfaces. Some aircraft had wing leading edges all in Dark Green. The upper surface colour demarcations were either hard or soft (feathered), but the upper/lower surface colour demarcation was invariably hard. In service, weathering often blurred hard darmarcations.

Serial numbers were painted in black numerals and letters below the wings, reading from the front on the left wing and the rear on the right. From 1978 the serial was moved to a new position below the inboard wing panels having previously used the full half-span. The serials were repeated on the rear fuselage sides in black numerals and characters. The serial's numerals were initially repeated at the top of the fin in white, a practice unusual on RAF aircraft, and this was often deleted by

squadrons. The numerals appeared in black at the bottom of the nose gear forward door on RAF FGR.2s.

Air-Superiority Grey
During 1974—77 the RAF's Phantoms were superseded in the tactical roles by Jaguars and were transferred to air defence duties. They retained their matt tactical camouflage. However, the UK-based Phantom's primary role is long-range interception, while the primary role of RAFG Phantoms is low-level, high-speed interception. Tactical camouflage is intended primarily for low-level attack operations over a wooded European landscape, and became increasingly inappropriate for the Phantom's new role. Of limited use in the early stages of transit to an operational area, its need at the home base was obviated by the provision of hardened aircraft shelters (HAS). Tactical camouflage is highly visible at high altitudes; with highly effective airborne interception radars, maximum concealment is essential to reduce the ability of an opponent to make and to hold visual acquisition — the 'eye-ball factor' still counts in modern fighter air combat.

The RAF had already begun investigating low-visibility air defence finishes, with uncertain results. The RAF's Lightning interceptors were in natural metal finish, which made them highly visible. In 1975 RAF Binbrook conducted air defence camouflage trials on Lightnings, including overall medium grey and overall light-blue grey. Initially a grey/green scheme was selected and applied from 1975, but a two-tone grey scheme was subsequently applied when further experiments had been conducted.

Re-camouflaging the RAF's air defence Phantoms, already in matt camouflage for tactical operations, was a less urgent priority than the Lightnings, but it became increasingly obvious that this scheme was unsuitable for air defence operations.

Investigations were begun and the first two Phantoms with toned-down grey schemes – based on those applied to the Lightnings – appeared in 1978. One of the Phantoms, XV418, went to RAF Wildenrath for trials with No 92 Squadron in RAFG.

Their overall finish was matt Light Aircraft Grey – as applied previously to under surfaces – although XV474 retained a black radome (XV418 did not). Underwing stencils were retained. The roundels were smaller than standard, and red/blue, like the fin flash, but in the six standard positions, over the old markings, whose outlines were still visible. The national markings' size and colours were modified over a period of months.

This scheme was rejected. A single grey created shadows which revealed shape. Medium Sea Grey for the upper surfaces was too dark, and diluting it produced the wrong effect. However, Light Aircraft Grey was acceptable for the under surfaces. Further studies led to the formulation of a standard scheme for toning-down Phantoms, devised by Mr P. J. Barley of RAF Farnborough. Three semi-matt (eggshell) colours were used. Two, Light Aircraft Grey and Medium Sea Grey, were standard BSC381C colours, 627 and 637 respectively. The third colour comprises twenty parts Light Aircraft Grey and one part Black and is officially named 'Barley Grey' after its inventor.

The entire undersurface is finished as before in Light Aircraft Grey. Medium Sea Grey is applied to the upper surfaces of the inboard wing panel. Barley Grey covers the fuselage sides and upper surfaces, the fin, rudder, stabilator upper surfaces and the entire radome. The upper surface colours return 4 inches on to the undersurfaces of the wing and stabilator leading edges.

The camouflage effect is produced by the subtle combination of light and medium greys, giving a uniform appearance to the aircraft's finish. Grey is a neutral colour which will reflect any surrounding colour if the correct degree of brilliance is selected – a 'chameleon' effect.

The greys have varied slightly from true specification, as they have come from several manufacturers – ICI, Dufay Titanine and International Pinchin-Johnson. The greys are applied with hard demarcation lines, but in service the finish soon deteriorates, making it difficult to distinguish them. In some lights these greys have a blue tone.

It took some two years to respray the entire RAF Phantom force in the three-greys scheme. It was applied to Phantoms as they went through IRAN (Inspection and Repair As Necessary) checks at No 30 Maintenance Unit at RAF St. Athan. The wrong grey has sometimes been applied, such as Light Aircraft Grey on fin, rudder, radome and access panels, or semi-gloss black radomes. Other aircraft have had Light Aircraft Grey intake lips, or leading edge.

Low-Visibility Markings

To complement the all-greys scheme, new, smaller, low-visibility fin flashes and Type B roundels are carried, the red reduced to a 'pink' and the blue to a 'lilac' or pale greyish-blue. These colours do not appear to equate to BSC381C colours, and were probably specially mixed, and will thus have a Ministry of Defence RDM 28A reference. The roundels are carried in the standard six positions; the upper wing roundels are some 8 inches further forward than those underwing.

Squadron emblems and checks were also toned-down and reduced. The position and sizes of unit badges, flashes and checks remained variable, as do individual code letters.

The serial on the rear fuselage, black on green/grey/grey aeroplanes, is white on all-grey aircraft; but the all-grey aeroplanes do not carry underwing serials. The serial numerals still appear in black on the nose gear front door.

On grey-green Phantoms, the plethora of stencils were mainly black, although some warnings were red; on grey Phantoms, stencils are generally white, and stand out more than on the grey-green finishes, but there have been and are many variations in position and style, and cases of omission or erosion. The wing root walkways are outlined in yellow and red.

Rescue markings and emergency markings and other NATO standard markings remain as before, in orange, black, white and red. Warning signs – ejection seat, warning triangles and the warning above the probe on the port nose – were red and white. Rescue markings were yellow or yellow and black. Rescue instruction panels and warnings are in German and English on RAFG Phantoms. Some Phantoms have one, two or three stencilled 'flashes' under the fin flash, or one, two or three small yellow pennants on the intakes, denoting armament systems update standards. A systems state panel is stencilled on the aft front undercarriage door.

Phantom Detail Colours

Phantom FGR.2 cockpit interiors, including the base colour of the instrument panels and consoles, are matt grey. The coaming under the windscreen and the inner canopy frames are matt black. Ejection seats are semi-gloss black, with black and yellow striped firing grips. The headrest, parachute and survival packs are matt buff or green, and harnesses are dull green, buff or grey.

Wheel well interiors, undercarriage door inner faces, undercarriage legs, wheel hubs, and pylons are gloss white. The doors have red edges, and many pylons have natural metal leading edges. The back faces of the main wheels are black. The nose wheel steering box is red.

The radome on disruptive-scheme aircraft was dull matt or semi-gloss blackish-brown. On low-visibility aircraft it is Barley Grey.

The dull natural metal areas on the rear fuselage are various tones depending on the metal or alloy, with areas of staining from heat and exposure. The titanium shields behind the jet effluxes are dark, with lighter aluminium shades under and above the stabilator, which includes the tail fairing from just in front of the stabilator pivot and, on some aircraft, the tail cone. The upper and lower surfaces of the stabilator are titanium and aluminium. The jet effluxes are dull brownish-black, and coated in soot.

The ILS blade aerials on the fin sides have, typically, been semi-gloss white with black leading edges. Generally, the front and rear of the RWR antenna fairing at the fin tip and the HF/VHF antenna on top of it have been matt light brown (buff), dark brown, brownish-black or black; typically, the front has been buff, pale cream or brownish-black and the rear brownish-black. The rest of the RWR fairing is treated as part of the camouflage surface.

The reconnaissance pods carried by the Phantom FGR.2 were Light Aircraft Grey. The SUU-23/A is Dark Green. Live AIM-7s, Sky Flashes and AIM-9s are basically white; training rounds are medium blue.

The Sergent Fletcher wing tanks were finished in Dark Green, Dark Sea Grey and Light Aircraft Grey camouflage on disruptive scheme aircraft. With the introduction of the low-visibility three-greys scheme, they were to be re-sprayed in Dark Sea Grey/Light Aircraft Grey, but, for some time, various finishes were worn – the original green/greys, overall Medium Sea Grey or Barley Grey, and some mixtures.

MODELLING RAFG IN 1/72nd SCALE

There are several mail order shops from whom goods hard to get locally can be bought. Modeltoys of Portsmouth offer a wide range by mail order, notably the excellent Modeldecals range. ED Models of Solihull import ranges of kits and accessories. They sell on the premises and by mail. Notable among their wares are the Model Technologies, C Scale, Airwaves, Chota Sahib and Almark decals ranges. Most of the specialist model companies sell by mail order, such as Airkit Enterprises of Erdington, Birmingham, Lead Sled of Ashburton, Devon, and PP Aeroparts of Bristol.

The modelling press records new releases of kits, conversion kits and accessories in advertisements, reviews and articles. For full details of the range of a manufacturer, buy their catalogue from a model shop or by mail. Smaller manufacturers have product lists often available for an SAE. Refer to the modelling press for addresses and prices.

PP Aeroparts stress that all their products are researched meticulously from source, and are of original design and manufacture; it is necessary to stress this because so many items are now pirated by unscrupulous persons!

Modern modelling is no longer limited to plastics. Specialist manufacturers use white metal, resin and etched brass as well as polystyrene components. The best way to assemble such items is with Isocyanoacylate glue – 'Superglue' – which will bond dissimilar products rapidly and strongly. It is also far less of a health risk than polysolvent.

For constructing white metal kits and accessories, it is useful to learn to solder with low-melt solder, for this gives a very strong bond and also fills the gaps between components as you go, rather than having to go back over the work with filler after assembling with glue. The correct kind of soldering iron, adjustable to specific low temperatures, must be used, together with good quality low-melt solder and flux, such as Carrs Red Label. A visit to a model railway shop should secure both products and advice on techniques.

The list of 1/72nd scale kits will allow all RAFG combat aircraft to be modelled, but it is not complete; while, conversely, some kits listed may be hard to obtain. Principally, only those kits providing directly the mark used by RAFG are listed; but where this is not available or in a poor rendering, other marks are given from which the modeller may be able to convert to the correct mark, either from his/her special skills or using a commercial conversion.

MISSILES

Model	Length in (mm)	Diameter in (mm)	Control Fin Span in (mm)	Launch Weight lb (kg)	Max. Range miles (km)	Mission Time sec	Tail Span in (mm)
AIM-9B	114.8 (2,830)	5 (127)	22 (559)	155 (70.4)	2 (3.2)	20	
AIM-9D	113 (2,870)	5 (127)	22.4 (630)	195 (88.5)	11 (17.7)	60	
AIM-9G	113 (2,870)	5 (127)	24.8 (630)	191 (86.6)	11 (17.7)	60	
AIM-9L	112.2 (2,050)	5 (127)	24.8 (630)	188 (85.3)	11 (17.7)	60	
AIM-7E-2	144 (3,660)	8 (203)	40 (1,020)	452 (228)	28 (44)	–	31.5 (800)
Sky Flash	145 (3,680)	8 (203)	40 (1,020)	425 (193)	31 (50)	–	31.5 (800)

AIM-9 Guidance

Model	Guidance	Sensor	Cooling	Look Angle°	Reticle Hz	Tracking °/sec
AIM-9B	IR	PbS	None	+1/−25	70	11
AIM-9D/G	IR	PbS	Nitrogen	+1/−40	125	12
AIM-9L	IR	InSb	Argon	ALASCA tilted	Fixed mirror	

1/72nd Scale Construction Kits

Bloodhound SAM and launcher	Airfix with Land Rover	Harrier GR.1	Lindberg	Jaguar A	Airfix
Bloodhound SAM and launcher	Airfix ditto in C-130	Harrier GR.1	Matchbox	Jaguar A, GR.1	Hasegawa
		Harrier GR.3	Airfix	Jaguar A, E, T.2	Frog/Novo
Buccaneer S.2B	Frog/Novo	Harrier GR.3	ESCI	Jaguar A, E, T.2	Heller/Humbrol
Buccaneer S.2B	Matchbox	Harrier GR.3	Fujimi	Jaguar GR.1	Airfix
		Harrier GR.3	Hasegawa	Jaguar GR.1	Matchbox
Canberra B(I).6/B.20	Airfix	Harrier T.4	Heller/Humbrol	Jaguar E, T.2	Hasegawa
Canberra PR.7	Frog	Harrier II/AV-8B (GR.5)	Italeri		
Canberra B(I).8/B.12	Frog/Novo			Javelin FAW.9/(R)	Frog/Novo
Canberra PR.9	Matchbox			Javelin T.3	Heller/Humbrol
Chipmunk	Airfix	Hunter F.6	Airfix	Lightning F.1A	Airfix reissue
		Hunter FGA.9	Airfix	Lightning F.3	Airfix reissue
		Hunter F.6	Central	Lightning F.6	Frog/Novo
Harrier GR.1	Airfix	Hunter FGA.9/F.5B	Frog/Novo	Lightning F.6	Hasegawa
Harrier GR.1	Hasegawa	Hunter F.6/T.7	Matchbox	Lightning F.2A/F.6	Matchbox
				Lightning T.55	Matchbox

Meteor F.3	Airfix	Tornado GR.1	ESCI	Swift FR.5	Rareplanes vacform
Meteor F.4	Frog	Tornado GR.1/F.2	Ravell		
Meteor F.8	Cruver	Tornado GR.1	Heller/Humbrol		

Other Scales Selection

1/144th Scale

Meteor F.8 — Frog
Meteor F.8/PR.10 — Rareplanes vac
Meteor NF.14 — Matchbox

Phantom FG.1/FGR.2 — Frog
Phantom FG.1/FGR.2 — Hasegawa
Phantom FG.1/FGR.2 — Matchbox
Phantom FG.1/FGR.2 — Revell
Phantom FG.1/FGR.2 — Fujimi Hi-Tech

Puma HC.1 — Airfix

Sabre, F-86A-5 — Matchbox: wing only
Sabre, F-86E — Cruver
Sabre, F-86E — Frog
Sabre, F-86E — PMS
Sabre, F-86F-30 — Hasegawa: modify wing
Sabre, F-86F — Heller: modify wing

Tornado — Airfix
Tornado — ESCI
Tornado — Italeri
Tornado — Monogram
Tornado GR.1 — Airfix

Vampire F.3 — Cruver
Vampire F.5 — Cruver
Vampire FB.5/.50 — Frog/Novo
Vampire FB.5 — Heller/Humbrol
Venom FB.1 — Aeroclub
Venom FB.4 — Aeroclub

Wessex Mk.1/Mk.31 (S58 Choctaw) — Frog
Wessex HU.5/HAS.31 — Matchbox

Whirlwind (S-55) — Airfix
Whirlwind Mk.I — Aristo Craft
Whirlwind Mk.I — Cruver
Whirlwind Mk.I — Polistil
Whirlwind (S-55) — Ruch
Whirlwind (S-55) — Sanwa
Whirlwind HAR.10 — Maintrack
Whirlwind HAR.10 — Britavia vacform
Whirlwind HAR.22 — Airfix

Swift F.4 — Hawk
Swift F.4 — Testors
Swift F.5 — ID Models vacform

Other Scales Selection

1/144th Scale
Buccaneer S.2B — Revell
Harrier GR.1 — Revell
Jaguar GR.1 — Revell
Tornado GR.1 — Revell

1/100th Scale
Buccaneer S.2B — Tamiya
Buccaneer S.2B — Revell
Jaguar GR.1 — Revell
Tornado GR.1 — Revell

1/50th Scale
SA.330 Puma — Heller/Humbrol

1/48th Scale
Chipmunk T.10 — Aeroclub vacform
Phantom FG.1/FGR.2 — Hasegawa Hi-Grade
Wessex HAS.3 — Revell
Swift FR.5/F.7 — Falcon vacform

1/32nd Scale
SA.330 Puma — Matchbox
Venom NF.3 — Matchbox

Camouflage and Insignia

1968–73 Tac: Gloss Dark Green/Medium Sea Grey/Light Aircraft Grey Type A roundels, equal-width red/white/blue, six positions; red/white/blue fin flashes.

1973–74 AD/Tac: Semi-Matt Dark Green/Medium Sea Grey/Light Aircraft Grey Type B roundels, equal-width red/blue, six positions; red/blue fin flashes.

1976 AD/Tac: Matt Dark Green/Medium Sea Grey/Light Aircraft Grey Type A roundels, equal-width red/white/blue, six positions; red/white/blue fin flashes.

1978 AD: Semi-Gloss Medium Sea Grey/Barley Grey/Light Aircraft Grey Tac: Matt Dark Green/Medium Sea Grey/Light Aircraft Grey Type B roundels, equal width light blue/light red.

Codes

Individual aircraft letters either side of the fin or rudder, white, red, or red/white, or white or yellow outline.

Squadron Markings

Insignia on the fins, and checks or flashes on either side of the intake cheeks on Phantoms or forward fuselages of other aeroplanes.

RAF Germany Colours and Codes for Modellers

Colour	BS*	FS595a**	Methuen	Humbrol Authentic	Xtracolor
Light Aircraft Grey	381C.627	36357	22(C-D)1	HX5	X15
Barley Grey	4800.18.B.21	36314	24(C-D)2	–	X17
Medium Sea Grey	381C.637	36270	22D3	HX4	X3
Dark Sea Grey	381C.638	–	21E3	HX2	X4
Dark Green	381C.641	–	30(F-G)2	HX1	X1
Insignia Pale Red	–	32356	11A5	Precision Paints	M29
Insignia Pale Blue	–	35450	23A4	Precision Paints	M30

On grey-green-grey aircraft — matt; on three-grey aircraft — semi-matt

*British building industry standard; **US Federal standard

47. A hangar-full of No 230 Squadron Puma HC.1s, with 'DE' revealing some interesting detail of the hub, intakes, interior and exit arrangements. (RAF Gütersloh)

48. An old-style RAF hangar accommodating Chinook HC.1s of No 18 Squadron. The 'whuppa whuppa bird' has considerably increased BAOR's tactical air logistic capability. No 18 disbanded on the Wessex HC.2 at Gütersloh in December 1980 and returned to Odiham. It began to re-form on the Chinook on 24 February 1982, but was soon deployed to the South Atlantic in support of Operation 'Corporate'. It returned to Odiham in depleted but highly-experienced condition, and its delayed return to Gütersloh eventually began in April 1983, officially taking up residence on 3 May 1983. (RAF Gütersloh)

49. Revealing photograph of No 18 Squadron Chinook HC.1 'BE'. The Chinook is a tried and tested design, developed through US experience in Korea, and honed in Vietnam. (RAF Gütersloh)

▼50

50. A Rapier unit's Land Rover unloads from Chinook HC.1 ZA675 'BB' of No 18 Squadron. The introduction of No 18's Chinooks has endowed RAFG with a previously lacking heavy

vertical lift transport capability. (RAFG)

51. Chinook ZA675 uses its centre hook for an underslung load of a 1-tonne Land Rover and

a Rapier Fire Unit of the RAF Regiment. The Chinook HC.1 can carry up to 28,000lb (12,700kg) on the centre hook. (RAFG)

52. RAFG's standard helicopter colours, displayed by No 18 Squadron Chinook HC.1 ZA708 'BK', is matt Black undersurfaces and Dark Green/Dark Sea Grey disruptive pattern upper surfaces. (RAF Gütersloh)

53. RAF Bruggen is home to four Tornado GR.1 squadrons, here ascending: Nos 9, 14, 17 and 31 Squadrons. Laarbruch houses Nos 2, 15, 16 and 20 Squadrons. During peacetime, for political reasons, in the three European Air Regions offensive forces are designated as national assets and assigned to the operational control of the parent nation. Defensive forces are designated as NATO assets and assigned to SACEUR. (Sgt R. J. Brewell, ABIPP, RAF Bruggen)

▲54　▼55　　　　　　　　　　　　　▲56

54. Three-quarters of a billion pounds sterling investment – the Bruggen Wing. Forty Tornado GR.1s and their eighty crew occupy the runway. Since the mid-1970s RAFG has twice re-equipped to meet the perceived threat from the Warsaw Pact: in the air, low-level, fast strike/attack aircraft, and, on the ground, swift-moving armour. RAFG has become a co-ordinated air force with a full range of roles and appropriate aircraft with which to carry out its missions. (Sgt G. Card, ABIPP, RAF Bruggen)

55. Two No 9 Squadron Tornado GR.1s demonstrate the type's great warload: counter-measures pods outboard, fuel tanks inboard, and eight 1,000lb HEMC bombs on the belly hardpoints. The TWOATAF Sector, covering 60,000 square miles, extends north to the Northern Region boundary, south to the French border and FOURATAF Sector boundary, and west to the United Kingdom Air Defence Region (UKADR) boundary in the North Sea. The Sector's eastern boundary is the East/West German border; in war, it would be a good deal further! The Tornado needs its long range and heavy load. (Sgt R. J. Brewell, ABIPP, RAF Bruggen)

56. Tornado 'AD' of No 9 Squadron lobs no fewer than eight 1,000lb bombs at the target on the RAFG oversea bombing ranges. It is equipped for flight-refuelling. From 1984 the multi-role Tornado began to replace both Jaguars and Buccaneers in FBSA and recce roles. (Sgt G. Card, ABIPP, RAF Bruggen)

57. Tornado GR.1 'AA' of No 9 Squadron at 'peacetime low altitude' shows off its overall Dark Green/Dark Sea Grey disruptive camouflage. The airframe is designed to give the performance required in ultra-low-level, high-threat operations. Support of land forces is the key to RAF Germany. (Sgt R. J. Brewell, ABIPP, RAF Bruggen)

58. 'DJ' of No 31 Squadron shows off the Tornado GR.1's great tail

57▲ 58▼

59▼

area, and larger ferry tanks. (RAFG)

59. No 31 Squadron Tornado GR.1 'DY' fitted with the new laser fairing. The Tornado's

weapons system will accommodate the full range of NATO stores from iron bombs to smart missiles, and the electronics suite will control all stages of a mission from start-up

through to weapons release and exit evasion manoeuvres. (Sgt R. J. Brewell, ABIPP, RAF Bruggen)

▲60 ▼61

▼62

60. Tornado 'DM' of No 31 Squadron over a snow-covered German plain. Unlike the Jaguar, the Tornado has full all-weather/day-night capability, reintroducing night attack, an option endowed by the Phantom but not available with the Jaguar. (BAe)

61. A battle Flight of four No 31 Squadron Tornadoes fly above the clouds. Their strike/attack role may demand a transit or return from a target at high altitude, but the formation would be spaced out over several thousand metres. (BAe)

62. Laarbruch houses four Tornado squadrons, Nos 2, 15, 16 (illustrated) and 20. With the level of air power committed to Central Europe, co-ordination between air forces is vital. There are therefore regular air exercises with Northern region, UKADR and FOURATAF units, and exchange basings with other NATO Europe air forces are undertaken to ensure that the structure is effective – notably TACEVALS. (BAe)

63. The Harrier GR.3 was developed from the GR.1 basically by fitting an uprated Pegasus 103 engine, and installing a Ferranti laser and marked-target seeker (LRMTS) in a 'thimble nose' which permits use of laser-guided bombs (LGBs). The GR.1A was an interim upgrade with Pegasus 102. This shot of a No 3 Squadron GR.3 in a shelter reveals much detail. (RAF Gütersloh)

64. A Harrier GR.3 of No 3 Squadron descends vertically – indicated by the positions of the nozzles. Unannounced TACEVALS (Tactical Evaluations) test the ability of a base to come to a war footing immediately, to carry out sustained air operations in the face of simulated air and ground attacks, and achieve assigned objectives; these are the most realistic war exercises mounted anywhere! They can be particularly gruelling for rough-living Harrier units. (RAFG)

65. Harrier GR.3 'E' of No 3 Squadron makes a rolling vertical descent – see the nozzles – which will enable it to keep its intake ahead of the dust and debris envelope, a technique which was developed during early V/STOL operations. (RAFG)

66. No 3 Squadron Harrier GR.3s XV781 'O', XV834 'J' and XV738 'B' on a practice bombing mission over the ranges (see the target wall beneath them), carrying combat fuel tanks, and CBLS on the centre-line pylon. The nearest aircraft, XV781, may only recently have been converted, from the thirty-first GR.1, because the laser nose is improperly camouflaged. (BAe)

▲ 65   ▼ 66

67. No 3 Squadron's Harrier XV738 'B' is a significant aeroplane. It was the first production GR.1, subsequently upgraded to GR.1A and then to GR.3. (BAe)

68. A No 4 Squadron Harrier GR.3 under camouflage netting in a clearing with the ladder and planking designed for the Harrier. The CBR of typical European fields is less than 4 per cent in winter and 5 per cent upwards in summer (CBR: California Load Bearing – the measure of load bearing and trafficability, with consolidated crushed rock giving 100 per cent). Thus, the Military Engineering Experimental Establishment, Hampshire, developed extruded aluminium planking for Harrier field operations. (RAFG)

▼ 67

▲69　▼70

▼71

69. A No 4 Squadron Harrier GR.3 'parked' in a small side-road between trees under camouflage netting. It demonstrates how effective camouflage can be, and the use that can be made of roads. (RAF Gütersloh)

70. Harrier GR.3 'E' of No 4 Squadron is guided from its off-road hide by groundcrew, wearing camouflage combat dress. The Harrier can operate from short lengths of road anywhere. (BAe)

71. Harrier GR.3 'E' of No 4 Squadron ascends with trees close by on either side. The Harrier's ability to operate from 'pop-up' positions close to the forward line of own troops (FLOT) makes it a unique, flexible and very efficient close support weapon – a true equivalent of artillery. (BAe)

72. Harrier GR.3 XZ135 'CP' of No 4 Squadron hovers in a clearing below treetop level. Throughout the 1980s the Harrier GR.3 has remained in the close-support inventory. The arrival of the new Harrier GR.5 is eagerly awaited. Its improved performance, weapons capability and survivability will upgrade RAFG's battlefield support and anti-armour capability for the first time in a decade. (RAFG)

73. A section of No 4 Squadron Harriers is manoeuvred up an unmetalled road beside a field. The Harrier can operate from firm ground such as this. The section is dispersed among the trees behind. Although infra-red recce and imaging systems may destroy the greatest part of camouflage's value, it nevertheless involves great effort in finding dispersed Harriers and minimizes an attacker's first pass success. (Sgt G. Card, ABIPP, RAF Bruggen)

74. When operating from dispersed sites, communication to air/land support co-ordinating authority is essential, effected by radio and despatch rider. The aeroplane is a Harrier T.4 two-seater, produced by lengthening the nose section for a second cockpit forward and raising the existing cockpit, and by adding a rear boom and increasing the fin base height to re-balance stability. The T.4 retains full combat capability. (RAF Gütersloh)

◀ 75 ▲ 76

75. Two RAF groundcrew remove rounds from a Harrier GR.3's port 30mm Aden cannon through the side access panel, while another refuels the aircraft through the ground refuelling point. The cannon's rear fairing has been removed, exposing the 100-round ammunition box. (RAF Gütersloh)

76. At a dispersed site, two groundcrew use a C type winch to lift a BL755 cluster bomb from a bomb trolley on to the ML No 119 ejector release unit (ERU) on the outboard pylon. The winch pivots on the pylon with a pylon adaptor; the wires from each arm attach to the sides of the store. The store is suspended from the

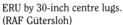

78 ▲

ERU by 30-inch centre lugs. (RAF Gütersloh)

77. Groundcrew arm a No 4 Squadron Harrier GR.3 with four BL755s. The last task will be to arm the Safety, Arming and Fusing Unit (SAFU) in the nose of each CBU, which will activate

the weapon at a predetermined point after release when it will disgorge 147 anti-armour/fragmentation bomblets in a devastating pattern. (RAF Gütersloh)

78. A groundcrewman services the laser nose of a No 3 Squadron

Harrier GR.3 in the field with the help of a tubular-metal trolley. For a tactical air force, ease and speed of maintenance and repair are vital components of maximum aggression. (BAe)

79. No 3 Squadron Harrier GR.3 XV801 'Y' undergoes an engine

change in the field. The wing has been removed, exposing the engine, which is then lifted out, complete with nozzles. A specialized gantry was developed to do this efficiently. (RAFG)

79 ▼

▲80 ▼81

80. More demanding Harrier maintenance is undertaken at the Harrier squadron's parent base, Gütersloh. Deep servicing or major work requires the involvement of No 431 Maintenance Unit at Bruggen, or BAe. Rolls-Royce overhaul and repair the Pegasus engine. (RAF Gütersloh)

81. At a distance of 300 metres, this decoy Harrier is sufficiently realistic to distract a tactical pilot flying at 450 knots or more at 20 metres altitude. Concentrating upon multiple system tasks, worried about SAMs and AAA, he has little time to identify targets before committing himself and releasing his warload – and may never realize that he has destroyed a model. (BAe)

82. Since 1983 the BAe Rapier has provided RAFG's short-range air defence (SHORAD). The trailer also forms the fire unit, a concept evolved for mobile war. Rapier's introduction to airfield defence during the late 1970s was part of the 'hardening-up' process. It made RAFG's bases hard to penetrate, while liberating interceptors from restrictive point defence duties. (RAF Gütersloh)

83. Chipmunk T.10 WG466 of the Berlin Flight flies over the Grunwald. The Flight exists to maintain Britain's right to overfly Berlin, and to keep the air routes open. (No 7 Flight, Army Air Corps)

84. Chipmunk T.10 WG486 courtesy of RAFG Gatow; Mil Mi-8 'Hip-C' courtesy of the GSFG. (Photo courtesy of No 7 Flight, Army Air Corps)

82 ▲   83 ▼

84 ▼

The *Fotofax* series

A new range of pictorial studies of military subjects for the modeller, historian and enthusiast. Each title features a carefully-selected set of photographs plus a data section of facts and figures on the topic covered. With line drawings and detailed captioning, every volume represents a succinct and valuable study of the subject. New and forthcoming titles:

Warbirds
F-111 Aardvark
P-47 Thunderbolt
B-52 Stratofortress
Stuka!
Jaguar
US Strategic Air Power:
   Europe 1942–1945
Dornier Bombers
RAF in Germany

Vintage Aircraft
German Naval Air Service
Sopwith Camel
Fleet Air Arm, 1920–1939
German Bombers of WWI

Soldiers
World War One: 1914
World War One: 1915
World War One: 1916
Union Forces of the American
   Civil War
Confederate Forces of the
   American Civil War
Luftwaffe Uniforms
British Battledress 1945–1967
   (2 vols)

Warships
Japanese Battleships, 1897–
   1945
Escort Carriers of World War
   Two
German Battleships, 1897–
   1945
Soviet Navy at War, 1941–1945
US Navy in World War Two,
   1943–1944
US Navy, 1946–1980 (2 vols)
British Submarines of World
   War One

Military Vehicles
The Chieftain Tank
Soviet Mechanized Firepower
   Today
British Armoured Cars since
   1945
NATO Armoured Fighting
   Vehicles
The Road to Berlin
NATO Support Vehicles

The *Illustrated* series

The internationally successful range of photo albums devoted to current, recent and historic topics, compiled by leading authors and representing the best means of obtaining your own photo archive.

Warbirds
US Spyplanes
USAF Today
Strategic Bombers, 1945–1985
Air War over Germany
Mirage
US Naval and Marine Aircraft
   Today
USAAF in World War Two
B-17 Flying Fortress
Tornado
Junkers Bombers of World War
   Two
Argentine Air Forces in the
   Falklands Conflict
F-4 Phantom Vol II
Army Gunships in Vietnam
Soviet Air Power Today
F-105 Thunderchief
Fifty Classic Warbirds
Canberra and B-57
German Jets of World War Two

Vintage Warbirds
The Royal Flying Corps in
   World War One
German Army Air Service in
   World War One
RAF between the Wars
The Bristol Fighter
Fokker Fighters of World War
   One
Air War over Britain, 1914–
   1918
Nieuport Aircraft of World War
   One

Tanks
Israeli Tanks and Combat
   Vehicles
Operation Barbarossa
Afrika Korps
Self-Propelled Howitzers
British Army Combat Vehicles
   1945 to the Present
The Churchill Tank
US Mechanized Firepower
   Today
Hitler's Panzers
Panzer Armee Afrika
US Marine Tanks in World War
   Two

Warships
The Royal Navy in 1980s
The US Navy Today
NATO Navies of the 1980s
British Destroyers in World
   War Two
Nuclear Powered Submarines
Soviet Navy Today
British Destroyers in World
   War One
The World's Aircraft Carriers,
   1914–1945
The Russian Convoys, 1941–
   1945
The US Navy in World War
   Two
British Submarines in World
   War Two
British Cruisers in World War
   One
U-Boats of World War Two
Malta Convoys, 1940–1943

Uniforms
US Special Forces of World
   War Two
US Special Forces 1945 to the
   Present
The British Army in Northern
   Ireland
Israeli Defence Forces, 1948 to
   the Present
British Special Forces, 1945 to
   Present
US Army Uniforms Europe,
   1944–1945
The French Foreign Legion
Modern American Soldier
Israeli Elite Units
US Airborne Forces of World
   War Two
The Boer War
The Commandos World War
   Two to the Present
Victorian Colonial Wars

A catalogue listing these series and other Arms & Armour Press titles is available on request from: Sales Department, Arms & Armour Press, Artillery House, Artillery Row, London SW1P 1RT.